Leaders
of the American Revolution

Dale Anderson

🌐 **WORLD ALMANAC® LIBRARY**

Please visit our web site at: www.worldalmanaclibrary.com
For a free color catalog describing World Almanac® Library's list of high-quality books
and multimedia programs, call 1-800-848-2928 (USA) or 1-800-387-3178 (Canada).
World Almanac® Library's fax: (414) 332-3567.

Library of Congress Cataloging-in-Publication Data

Anderson, Dale, 1953-
    Leaders of the American Revolution / by Dale Anderson.
        p. cm. — (World Almanac Library of the American Revolution)
    Includes bibliographical references and index.
    ISBN 0-8368-5931-6 (lib. bdg.)
    ISBN 0-8368-5940-5 (softcover)
    1. United States—Politics and government—1775-1783—Juvenile literature. 2. United States—History—Revolution,
1775-1783—Juvenile literature. 3. United States—History—Revolution, 1775-1783—Biography—Juvenile literature.
4. Statesmen—United States—Biography—Juvenile literature. 5. Generals—United States—Biography—Juvenile literature.
6. Statesmen—Great Britain—Biography—Juvenile literature. 7. Generals—Great Britain—Biography—Juvenile literature.
8. United States—History—Revolution, 1775-1783—British forces—Juvenile literature. I. Title. II. Series.
E210.A5184   2005
973.3'092'2—dc22   2005041641

First published in 2006 by
World Almanac® Library
A Member of the WRC Media Family of Companies
330 West Olive Street, Suite 100
Milwaukee, WI 53212 USA

Produced by Discovery Books
Editor: Sabrina Crewe
Designer and page production: Sabine Beaupré
Photo researcher: Sabrina Crewe
Maps and diagrams: Stefan Chabluk
Consultant: Andrew Frank, Assistant Professor of History, Florida Atlantic University
World Almanac® Library editorial direction: Mark J. Sachner
World Almanac® Library editor: Alan Wachtel
World Almanac® Library art direction: Tammy West
World Almanac® Library production: Jessica Morris

Photo credits: CORBIS: pp. 16, 19, 32; The Granger Collection: pp. 5, 13, 17, 18, 21, 25, 27, 29, 31, 35, 37, 38 (bottom),
40, 41, 42, 43; Independence National Historical Park: cover, title page; North Wind Picture Archives: pp. 7, 8, 9, 11, 12,
15, 22, 28, 38 (top).

Printed in Canada

1 2 3 4 5 6 7 8 9 09 08 07 06 05

*Front cover: Thomas Jefferson was one of the greatest leaders of the American Revolution. He went on to become the
United States' second vice president and then, from 1801 to 1809, the nation's third president. This portrait of Jefferson
was painted by Charles Willson Peale in 1791–1792.*

*Title page: James Peale painted this portrait of George Washington on horseback in about 1790. He based the
portrait on a work by his brother, Charles Willson Peale—the faces of both the brothers can be seen on the left,
behind Washington. In the background on the right are Revolutionary soldiers, one carrying a French flag.*

Contents

In 1776, the thirteen British **colonies** along the eastern coast of North America declared themselves independent of Britain. The colonists were already fighting British soldiers in protest at British policies. In 1781, the British surrendered to American forces, and, in 1783, they formally recognized the colonies' independence.

A New Nation

The movement from colonies to independence, known as the American Revolution, gave birth to a new nation—the United States of America. Eventually, the nation stretched to the Pacific Ocean and grew to comprise fifty states. Over time, it was transformed from a nation of farmers into an industrial and technological giant, the world's richest and most powerful country.

An Inspiration to Others

The American Revolution was based on a revolution of ideas. The people who led the American Revolution believed that the purpose of government was to serve the people, not the reverse. They rejected rule by monarchs and created in its place a **republic**. The founders of the republic later wrote a **constitution** that set up this form of government and guaranteed people's basic rights, including the right to speak their minds and the freedom to worship as they wished.

The ideals on which the United States of America was founded have inspired people all around the world ever since. Within a few years of the American Revolution, the people of France had risen up against their monarchy. Over time, the people of colonies in Central

*Patriot leaders formed a temporary government, the Continental **Congress**, to give direction to the colonies as they moved toward independence. This print shows the Congress appointing George Washington (standing, center) to lead the Continental army in June 1775.*

and South America, in Asia, and in Africa followed the U.S. example and rebelled against their position as colonists. Many former colonies have become independent nations.

The Role of Leaders

Thousands of Americans took part in actions against British government **policies** in the 1760s and 1770s. Intelligent and committed leaders gave those actions shape and direction. Some leaders organized protests, while others wrote and made speeches. British government leaders, meanwhile, led the response to those actions.

The war that broke out in 1775 was a result of steps—and missteps—taken by leaders on both sides of the Atlantic. Political leaders shaped the war effort from the early days until its end in 1783. Leading figures in the American Revolution, calling themselves **Patriots**, formed a new national government to direct the war.

Military Leaders

The war, of course, could not be won without military success. The Patriots needed military leaders who could carry out a war against Britain, one of the world's greatest powers. British military leaders, meanwhile, were equally important in the effort to put down the rebellion and try to keep America under Britain's control.

CHAPTER ONE

Patriot Political Leaders

Many Patriot political leaders had experience in the rough world of colonial government. Some had held town offices, and others had been elected to colonial **legislatures** before the war.

Men of Wealth and Property

American society in the 1700s was divided into several social classes. The upper class was wealthy either because of vast landholdings or profitable business dealings. Many landowners came from large families that had been powerful and influential in their colonies for several generations. The majority of Patriot leaders came from those families that dominated colonial society. They were men of wealth, property, and education.

The Enlightenment

Many Patriot leaders were deeply influenced by the political ideas of the **Enlightenment**. The **philosophers** who led the Enlightenment movement said that all people had the same basic rights. British philosopher John Locke called them the rights to "life, liberty, and property."

Enlightenment leaders also said that humans formed societies on the basis of an agreement they called a social contract. People gave power to their government so they could enjoy peace and prosperity. When a government threatened their rights, that social contract was broken, and the people had the right to create a new government. These were the ideas that drove Patriot leaders, such as Thomas Jefferson, in their movement for independence from Britain.

Thomas Jefferson (1743–1826)

Before, during, and for many years after the Revolution, Thomas Jefferson's words and actions shaped the United States of America. His ideas about liberty and the role of government continue to influence American society today.

Thomas Jefferson reads over the Declaration of Independence by candlelight before presenting it to his fellow members of the Continental Congress.

Born in Virginia, Thomas Jefferson was the son of rich landowners. He studied law, but he practiced for only three years, from 1767 to 1770. From 1769, Jefferson represented Virginians in the colony's legislature, the House of Burgesses. He was sent as a **delegate** to the Continental Congress in 1775. Jefferson was a gifted writer and was chosen to write the Declaration of Independence. Returning to Virginia in 1776, Jefferson spent the next years pushing reforms that would reflect the ideals of a republic—separating church and state, establishing public schools, and ending the slave trade. At the same time, he was a wealthy plantation owner and slave owner himself. Jefferson served as governor of Virginia from 1779 to 1781.

After the Revolution ended, Jefferson returned to the Congress. In 1785, he went to France as U.S. ambassador. In 1789, George Washington appointed Jefferson as secretary of state. Jefferson went on to become vice president in 1797 and then the third president of the United States in 1801. While in office, he arranged to buy the Louisiana Territory from France, nearly doubling the nation's size. After Jefferson retired to his estate in Virginia, he founded the University of Virginia. He died on the same day (the fiftieth anniversary of the Declaration of Independence) as John Adams, having made an unsurpassed contribution to American independence and the founding of the United States.

Rising to Prominence

Not everyone who became a leader during the American Revolution was from the wealthiest, landowning class. The colonies had a thriving community of merchants, professionals, and business owners that yielded several influential figures.

Benjamin Franklin was the son of a candle maker. Through hard work, immense talent, and a shrewd mind, he grew to become a successful businessman and a widely popular leader. John Adams, the son of a farmer, used his college education and a career in law to become one of the most important figures in the Patriot cause. Alexander Hamilton made his way from the West Indies to New York just before the Revolution. He gained

John Adams (1735–1826)

One of the earliest voices in favor of American independence was John Adams. He graduated from Harvard University when he was twenty and began working as a teacher. Adams found he preferred the law and became a successful lawyer. When unrest began in Boston, he quickly became involved in anti-British protests. Adams wrote several pamphlets protesting British **taxes** on the colonies. He served in both the First and Second Continental Congresses and worked tirelessly to convince other members to support independence and to help the Patriots win the war. While doing this work, Adams endured many years of separation from his wife, Abigail, and their children. Adams also spent some years in Europe, representing the United States in the Netherlands, France, and Britain. In the 1790s, he was the first vice president of the United States and then the country's second president. In 1801, he retired to his home in Massachusetts, where he lived surrounded by books and full of ideas until his death on July 4, 1826.

attention first by writing pamphlets and then by organizing a military company. All these men contributed to the cause during the Revolution and went on to become national leaders after the war ended.

Networks of Patriots

Paul Revere is remembered for his ride through Massachusetts on the night of April 18–19, 1775. That night, he alerted Patriots in towns from Cambridge to Concord that British soldiers were on the march to seize Patriot military supplies in Concord. These warnings led the local **militias** to fight the British at the Battle of Lexington and Concord.

Revere, however, played a far more important role in the years leading up to that night. He was a key leader of a network of storekeepers, crafts-people, and other workers in Boston who supported the Patriot cause. They were the people who made up the bulk of the protestors that Patriots

Before the Revolution, Paul Revere was a courier for the Patriots in Massachusetts. He traveled by horseback to take messages and distribute pamphlets around the colony.

relied on for public demonstrations against the British. These groups—called Sons of Liberty in many places—and leaders such as Revere were found throughout the colonies. Through them, ordinary people made their voices heard.

Limits to Democracy

In the 1700s, however, there were limits in society that prevented real equality. Patriots believed that "the people" had the right to choose leaders, but those people did not include everyone. Women were excluded from voting, as were Native Americans and African Americans. (In fact, the right to own slaves was one of the freedoms that Patriots were fighting for.) There were also poor people—servants and laborers—who did not have equal political rights. Many Patriot leaders thought that only citizens with property had a stake in society. Several worried that complete democracy

Misled People

"[The people] should have as little to do as may be [possible] about the government. They [lack] information and are constantly liable to be misled."

Patriot leader Roger Sherman of Connecticut, 1787

Tea for Freedom

"Stand firmly resolved
and bid Grenville see
That rather than Freedom,
we'll part with our Tea."

Patriot woman urging a boycott of British tea

would threaten society as a whole and their own financial interests in particular. For many years, only white, male property owners were allowed to vote.

Women Lead the Boycotts

Although they had no voice in politics, women influenced the Revolution in other ways. Before the war, colonists **boycotted** British goods to protest the taxes they were forced to pay on those goods. Women led this effort, for they were the ones who had to make cloth and homemade teas. They formed groups, such as the Daughters of Liberty, to organize support for the cause. The women achieved impressive results. The women of Middletown, Massachusetts, for instance, produced more than 20,000 yards (18,000 meters) of cloth in 1769. The industrious women of Lancaster, Pennsylvania, made nearly 35,000 yards (32,000 m) in one year.

Temporary Legislatures

When the fighting began, most of the

BOSTON, December 2, 1773.

WHEREAS it has been reported that a Permit will be given by the Custom-House for Landing the Tea now on Board a Veffel laying in this Harbour, commanded by Capt. HALL: THIS is to Remind the Publick, That it was folemnly voted by the Body of the People of this and the neighbouring Towns affembled at the Old-South Meeting-Houfe on Tuefday the 30th Day of *November*, that the faid Tea never fhould be landed in this Province, or pay one Farthing of Duty: And as the aiding or affifting in procuring or granting any fuch Permit for landing the faid Tea or any other Tea fo circumftanced, or in offering any Permit when obtained to the-Mafter or Commander of the faid Ship, or any other Ship in the fame Situation, muft betray an inhuman Thirft for Blood, and will alfo in a great Meafure accelerate Confufion and Civil War: This is to affure fuch public Enemies of this Country, that they will be confidered and treated as Wretches unworthy to live, and will be made the firft Victims of our juft Refentment.

The PEOPLE.

N. B. Captain *Bruce* is arrived laden with the fame deteftable Commodity: and 'tis peremptorily demanded of him, and all concerned, that they comply with the fame Requifitions.

A 1773 handbill warns the people of Boston to have nothing to do with imported British tea. Anybody who does so, it says, will be considered a public enemy.

royal governors fled and the rest were forced out of office. By the end of 1775—the first year of the American Revolution—Patriots were in control of all the colonial legislatures.

The first governing bodies formed by the Patriots were temporary. They consisted of members of town councils and colonial assemblies who created new legislatures during the American Revolution, when British colonial governments broke down. These Patriot legislatures chose and sent delegates to the Continental Congress.

Seats in the self-appointed legislatures were fairly distributed according

Great Men

"This assembly is like no other that ever existed. Every man in it is a great man—an orator, a critic, a statesman, and therefore every man upon every question must show his oratory, his criticism, and his political abilities. The consequence of this is that business is drawn and spun out to immeasurable length."

Patriot leader John Adams of Massachusetts, describing the Second Continental Congress and its delegates, June 1775

to population and were, therefore, more representative of western regions than the old colonial assemblies had been. The Westerners tended to be farmers and recent settlers struggling for survival, very unlike the rich men who represented older settlements.

Even before the Declaration of Independence, Patriot legislatures began to write constitutions for their colonies, soon to be states. After the constitutions were completed and approved, they elected new state governors, legislators, and other officials. These were, quite often, the same men who had served in the

Patrick Henry (standing, left), a leading Patriot, used the Virginia legislature as a platform from which to encourage independence from Britain. He made famous speeches there in 1765 and 1775.

We Must Fight

"If we wish to be free—if we mean to preserve . . . those inestimable privileges for which we have been so long contending . . . we must fight!"

Patrick Henry, speech to Virginia legislature, March 23, 1775

Revolutionary Writings

Some Patriots became leaders through their words. Both before and during the Revolution, writers aired their views in newspapers and published essays that ranged from ten to fifty pages. In the days before television and radio, the circulation of written material was the only way to reach large numbers of people. The impact of these writings, therefore, was huge.

Some writers gained influence with their arguments for the Patriot cause. Thomas Jefferson, John Adams, Benjamin Franklin, and Paul Revere all became leaders in part because of their writings. A few, such as Thomas Paine, created a sensation with their words. Paine's 1776 pamphlet, *Common Sense*, made many colonists consider whether they really wanted or needed to be under the rule of a king in a distant country.

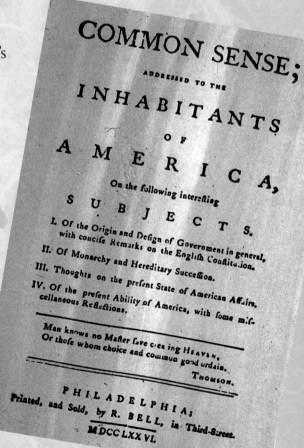

Writers often used harsh language to criticize opponents. One pamphlet called officials in the British government "court-locusts." Another said that British tax officials grasped for money with "long claws like eagles." Britain's supporters, mean- while, were equally vicious. One pro-British writer blasted the Patriots as "evil-minded and ill- disposed persons."

CHAPTER TWO

Patriot Military Leaders

Most Patriot military leaders had some experience in the militias, the forces in the colonies made up of citizen soldiers. A few had been officers in European armies, which gave them more formal military training.

Military Experience

The Revolution began only twelve years after the end of the French and Indian War. In that conflict, the British army and American militias fought the French army and its Native American allies. George Washington and Daniel Morgan of Virginia, Israel Putnam of Connecticut, and John Stark of New Hampshire had all led units of various sizes in the French and Indian War. Many Patriots led militia units after the war, too. Morgan and Stark used their leadership experience to get the best out of untrained militia troops, becoming effective leaders in the field. Both won battles when they were given independent command, and both also led their men well under other officers. Washington, meanwhile, wanted disciplined troops, and he trained the Continental army to be a match for British regulars.

Resourceful Commanders

On occasion, commanders of **regiments** personally led their troops into battle. Some generals and other officers died in combat, and others suffered wounds. Being an officer was not a ticket to safety.

Some of the Patriots' top commanders had no prior experience, but they became brave and resourceful leaders during the course of the

John Stark (center, in blue hat and white breeches) was a New Hampshire militia leader. His greatest victory against the British was at the Battle of Bennington, shown here, which took place in present-day New York state in 1777.

Mortally Wounded

"[General Hugh Mercer] immediately formed his men, with great courage, and poured a heavy fire in upon the enemy, but they being greatly superior in number returned the fire and charged bayonets, and their onset was so fierce that Gen. Mercer fell mortally wounded and many of his officers were killed."

Militia captain Thomas Rodney, describing the Battle of Princeton, 1777

Revolution. Benedict Arnold, for instance, was an inspiring leader of the Patriots until he became a traitor and joined the British. Nathanael Greene was another able commander with no prior experience. When he joined the militia in 1774, it was as a private. By the next year, however, officials in Rhode Island named him a general, and he commanded well during the war.

BICKERSTAFF's BOSTON ALMANACK, For the Year of our REDEMPTION, 1 7 7 8.

Being the Second Year of AMERICAN INDEPENDENCE. And the Second after LEAP-Year, Calculated for the Meredian of BOSTON, Lat. 42' 25° N. CONTAINING, besides what is neceffary in an Almanack, a Variety of ufeful and inftructing Pieces.

The GLORIOUS WASHINGTON and GATES.

Calculated by BENJAMIN WEST, a Student in Aftronomy, at Providence, and Author of this Almanack for twelve Years paft, except thofe falfe Editions printed by Mycall, of Newbury, for 76, and by Boyle and Draper and Phillips, of Bofton, for 77 : The Author of this genuine Copy never had any Connexions with thofe Printers.

DANVERS : Printed by E. RUSSELL, at his Printing-Office, late the Bell-Tavern. (Pr. 12/. per Dozen and 1/. 6d. fingle.)

The Boston Almanac *for 1778 featured a dedication to "The Glorious Washington and Gates" after Gates's victory at Saratoga. General Gates was disgraced two years later.*

Appointing Leaders

State governments named militia commanders, while the Continental Congress appointed generals to the Continental army. Officers were often chosen partly because of personal friendships or for political reasons. Virginian George Washington, for instance, was named commander in chief of the Continental army in 1775. The Congress wanted to show that the struggle was not just a New England effort, but one that involved the more southern colonies, too.

Disappointing Leaders

Charles Lee and Horatio Gates had both served in the British army before the war. Much was expected of both, but neither lived up to their promise. Lee proved unreliable in the field and insubordinate to Washington. In 1778, he was **court-martialed** and suspended for a year, and in 1780 the Congress dismissed him from the Continental army.

Gates's army defeated the army of General John Burgoyne in the fall of 1777 at Saratoga. The Congress was greatly impressed with Gates as a result (although historians still debate whether it was his leadership or that

Wretched Army

"When I came to the army I found it in a most wretched condition. The officers had lost all confidence in the general, and the troops all their discipline."

Nathanael Greene, on taking command of the southern Continental army, 1780

of Arnold and other commanders that really won the battle). Some members of the Congress wanted Gates to replace Washington as overall commander of the army. In August 1780, however, Gates suffered a humiliating defeat at Camden, South Carolina, and he was removed from command.

Power Conflicts

Washington and the Congress often struggled over decisions about appointments. Early in the war, Washington was angry when the Congress promoted some officers over those he supported. In 1780, he had wanted to put Nathanael Greene, rather than Horatio Gates, in charge of the southern army. After Gates's defeat at Camden, the Congress agreed that Greene should be put in command.

Foreign Officers in the Continental Army

Several foreign soldiers joined the Continental army and became leaders and heroes. They were inspired by Enlightenment ideals, the desire to fight the British, and dreams of glory. Gilbert du Motier, the Marquis de Lafayette, a young Frenchman, was inexperienced when he arrived, but he became a skilled general. In the fall of 1781, he effectively pushed British troops under General Charles Cornwallis toward the city of

Some junior Patriot officers later rose to great prominence. James Monroe of Virginia served for three years in the Continental army and took part in several battles. After the war, he held many different offices, including that of U.S. president from 1817 to 1825.

Yorktown, Virginia. French and American troops **besieged** the British army there until it surrendered.

The German officer Friedrich von Steuben was vital to the training of the Continental army. Two Patriot officers, German Johann de Kalb and the Pole Casimir Pulaski, both died in the Revolution and became heroes of the cause. Thaddeus Kosciuszko, another Pole, worked as a military engineer. In that role, he planned the

In the late winter of 1778, Friedrich von Steuben (right, in long coat) began drilling Continental army soldiers in their camp at Valley Forge, Pennsylvania. His efforts taught them the basic skills of soldiering and helped make them a better fighting force.

fortifications that helped produce a Patriot victory at Saratoga in 1777.

The French Commanders

In 1778, France became an ally of the new United States. In 1780, French military forces arrived to support the Continental army against the British. While their help was valuable, the alliance was not always smooth.

French cooperation, however, helped win the war. The leader of French forces in America was Jean Baptiste de Vimeur, the Comte de Rochambeau. In 1781, Washington and Rochambeau devised a plan for a combined French-American attack on British troops in Virginia. The successful effort led to the Patriot victory at the Battle of Yorktown, where the British surrendered to the allies.

Another French commander, Admiral François de Grasse, was instrumental in the victory at Yorktown. His ships brought soldiers to Virginia and fought off a British fleet that had come to rescue British soldiers trapped on the Yorktown peninsula. Although they entered the war late, these French commanders provided crucial support for the Patriots in the American Revolution.

Gilbert du Motier, the Marquis de Lafayette (1757–1834)

The Marquis de Lafayette was born into an aristocratic family in France. Eager to help the Patriots, he sailed for America in 1777 and offered his services. When Lafayette agreed to pay his own expenses, the Congress named him a general and sent him off to join Washington's army. During the war, Lafayette proved a good soldier and leader of men, and he donated large sums of his own money to help the cause. He and Washington became close friends. Back in France, Lafayette remained committed to republican ideals and played a role in the early years of the French Revolution (1789–1799). When rebels took control of France and began killing nobles, however, he fled the country. Lafayette was eventually able to return to France in 1800, but his wealth was gone. He returned to the United States in 1824, touring the country as a hero. Congress repaid him for his huge financial contribution to the American Revolution.

CHAPTER THREE

The Life of Washington

With his military leadership during the war, his political leadership afterward, and his moral leadership throughout, George Washington earned the name "Father of His Country." He made mistakes, and he faced heavy criticism at times. But Washington was, as one biographer calls him, "the indispensable man."

Washington's Youth

Washington was born in 1732, the younger son of a Virginia landowner. His father died when he was only eleven, and the main family home at

The Cherry Tree Myth

One of the most famous stories about Washington is untrue. After Washington's death, Mason Weems wrote a biography of him that aimed to set a good example for children. Weems claimed that, as a child, Washington cut down a cherry tree on the family estate. When questioned by his father, the young boy confessed, saying, "I can't tell a lie." The story Weems invented was later placed in a popular textbook, and millions of Americans came to believe it.

George Washington gained leadership experience in the French and Indian War of 1754–1760. This print shows him (right, on horseback) directing troops at the Battle of the Monogahela in July 1755.

Mount Vernon, Virginia, passed into the hands of George's older brother, Lawrence. After his father's death, George Washington spent his childhood with his mother, partly at Mount Vernon and partly at another family home, which he had inherited. He went to school only until about age fifteen.

In his late teens, Washington became a **surveyor**. This experience in studying land may have helped him later when he led armies in battle. In 1751, he was infected with smallpox. He survived the deadly disease and gained lifelong immunity to it as a result. The following year, Lawrence Washington died, and George inherited Mount Vernon.

Washington in the French and Indian War

In 1752, Washington became a major in the Virginia militia. At the time, the French and British were competing for land in North America. In 1754, the French and Indian War began. Washington served ably in the war until 1758, when he resigned his militia commission.

Washington and his wife Martha (above) lived at Mount Vernon, Virginia, after their marriage. They raised Martha's two children from her previous marriage and, later, two of her grandchildren.

Planter and Politician

Back in civilian life, Washington married Martha Dandridge Custis, a young and wealthy widow with many slaves and landholdings even larger than his own. The couple began living at Mount Vernon. Washington was an able farmer and carefully built up his family farms and plantations.

Washington was elected several times to the Virginia legislature.

He adopted the anti–British stance of many other plantation owners and was clear-sighted enough to see that continued protests would eventually lead to war. In September 1774, Virginia sent Washington and six others to the First Continental Congress in Philadelphia. After the meeting ended and he returned to Virginia, Washington began training militia troops.

Unequal to the Command

"Lest some unlucky event should happen . . . I beg it may be remembered, by every gentleman in this room, that I, this day, declare with the utmost sincerity, I do not think myself equal to the command I am honored with."

*George Washington
to the Continental Congress,
June 16, 1775*

Commander in Chief

When he appeared at the Second Continental Congress in May 1775, Washington wore his Virginia militia uniform. He aimed to show that Virginia was ready to fight if needed. But the move also reminded other delegates of Washington's military experience. In June 1775, when the Continental Congress decided to form the Continental army, it named Washington as its commander in chief. Washington accepted the post but declined to receive any salary, asking only to be reimbursed for his expenses.

At first glance, Washington's performance in the Revolution seems dismal. From the time he took command in 1775 until the British surrender at Yorktown in 1781, he won only two battles, those at Trenton and Princeton in the winter of 1776–1777. He lost all other battles and was forced to surrender the largest cities in America—New York and Philadelphia—to the British. Washington's battle plans were often far too complicated to succeed on the battlefield itself.

Moments of Excellence

Washington excelled at some important moments during the Revolution. Crossing the Delaware River on Christmas night in 1776 to attack the enemy in Trenton, New Jersey, was a brilliant move that some historians say saved the Revolution. Washington also rallied the troops at Monmouth in June 1778, preventing a terrible defeat. Most effective was the plan in 1781 to move American and French forces from the New York area to Yorktown, Virginia, to surround the British army there.

Love and Esteem

"The merit of restoring the day . . . is due to the General, and his conduct was such throughout the affair as has greatly increased my love and esteem for him."

John Laurens, aide to General Washington, after the Battle of Monmouth, 1778

An Inspiring Leader

Washington, however, provided stalwart and inspiring leadership, even in the worst of times. And he had a clear **strategy** for achieving the Patriot's goal of independence—keep the Continental army alive. As long as they suffered no devastating defeat, as long as they still had soldiers in the field, the Patriots could resist the British, and the dream of independence had a chance. Washington aimed to avoid a major battle that could destroy his army. If avoiding that battle meant retreating, he was willing to take that action, even if others viewed a retreat as cowardly or dishonorable.

Beloved Commander

Most of Washington's officers were devoted to him. When some leaders suggested replacing Washington, General Daniel Morgan said he would serve under no one else.

Continental army general Johann de Kalb said, "I look upon him as the sole defender of his country's cause."

One of Washington's most important actions came late in the war. In March 1783, before the peace was final, some officers threatened to abandon the army. Washington assembled his officers and, in a moving speech, urged them not to rebel. His appeal ended the mutiny.

In December of 1783, Washington gave up his commission as commander in chief and looked forward to rest and retirement. Only fifty-one years old, he was very tired.

Nation in Crisis

By 1787, the nation was in a crisis. Many leaders felt the need to have a stronger national government and wanted to hold a meeting in Philadelphia to discuss the idea. Washington's decision to attend that meeting—the Constitutional Convention—was a key factor in getting people to accept a constitution that created a stronger national government and the office of president. Many people believed he would be the first president, and they believed that he would not abuse his powers.

The First President

As expected, Washington was chosen as the first U.S. president in 1789. Through eight years in office, he

Greatly loved and admired by his fellow citizens, Washington was inaugurated as president of the United States on April 30, 1789 at Federal Hall in New York City. On the balcony with other government leaders, he is shown bowing to the crowd assembled below.

steered a difficult course. He backed plans that helped improve the U.S. economy, and he avoided taking sides in a new war between Britain and France. When farmers in western Pennsylvania rebelled over **federal** taxes, Washington personally led an army to quash the rebellion and show the rebels that the nation's laws had to be obeyed.

Washington grew increasingly tired during his presidency, not only because of his advancing age but also because of fighting within his government. In 1796, Washington announced that he would not accept a third term. The next year, he finally went home to Mount Vernon, where he died in 1799.

First in War and Peace

"First in war, first in peace, first in the hearts of his fellow citizens."

Congressman Henry Lee,
House of Representatives,
after George Washington's death, 1799

CHAPTER FOUR

Loyalist Leaders

White Americans who supported the British during the American Revolution are known as **Loyalists**. There were also many Native Americans and African Americans who took the British side, but the term Loyalists is used here to mean the former colonists who wanted to remain as British subjects. Many top officials in the colonies before the war—including governors and senior tax officials—stayed loyal to Britain when the conflict began.

Before the War

In the 1760s and 1770s, even before the Revolution began, Loyalists took part in the war of words carried out in newspapers and pamphlets. Many agreed with Patriots that colonists had certain rights as British subjects. They did not always agree that British policies violated those rights, however, and believed the

Many Tyrants

"For one lawful ruler, many tyrants we've got,
Who force young and old to their wars, to be shot,
With their hunting shirts and rifle guns.
Our good King, God speed him! never used men so,
We then could speak, act, and like freemen could go,
But committees enslave us, our liberty's gone,
Our trade and church murdered; our country's undone,
By hunting shirts and rifle guns."

"The Rebels," Loyalist song, 1778

British government could be reasoned with. Loyalists also clung to the order and stability that British rule provided. They were afraid of what would happen if the Revolution succeeded.

Fear of Violence

Loyalists decried actions like the Boston Tea Party of 1773, during which Patriots dumped cases of British tea into Boston Harbor to protest a British tax on tea. Their disapproval was even stronger when Patriots engaged in violent protests. Colonial officials who were also Loyalists had another reason to dislike violent protests—the violence was often aimed at them. Patriot groups often **looted** the officials' homes. Sometimes, they also beat or **tarred and feathered** officials.

Loyalist Governors

Those Loyalists who were in positions of power tried to suppress protests and put down the revolts, but their actions often made the situation worse. It was Thomas Hutchinson, the royal governor of Massachusetts, who insisted that British tea be landed in Boston in 1773, against the wishes of Bostonians, and that the British tax on the tea be enforced. This insistence set the stage for the Boston Tea Party.

Loyalist officials were targets of Patriot hostility before and during the American Revolution. This print shows a scene in 1765, where one tax official (top) is strung up on a "Liberty Pole," and another (bottom) is about to be tarred and feathered.

Thomas Hutchinson (1711–1780)

Thomas Hutchinson (right) is warned by Patriot Samuel Adams to withdraw British soldiers from Boston after the Boston Massacre of 1770, when British soldiers first killed rebellious colonists.

Thomas Hutchinson was born in Boston into a prosperous merchant family. He went to Harvard University at the age of twelve and graduated when he was sixteen. Hutchinson was in business until 1737, when he entered politics. He was named as lieutenant governor of Massachusetts in 1758 and as the colony's top judge two years later. Hutchinson did not agree with all the taxes imposed by the British in the 1760s, but he worked dutifully to enforce them. That work, along with his practice of giving government jobs to relatives, earned him the hatred of Patriots. When Boston crowds protested taxes created by the Stamp Act in 1765, they vandalized Hutchinson's home.

As royal governor—a post he gained in 1770—Hutchinson became a focal point of Patriot criticism. Tension and violence in the colony increased, and, in 1774, Hutchinson was replaced as governor by British general Thomas Gage. Hutchinson sailed for Britain, where he spent the rest of his life as an exile from the United States.

William Franklin—royal governor of New Jersey and son of Patriot leader Benjamin Franklin—supported the British when the war began. In June 1776, Patriots in New Jersey formed a temporary government and ordered William Franklin's arrest. Franklin was held by Patriots as a prisoner for more than two years.

Loyalist Leaders in Battle

During the war, in their fight to maintain British rule, some Loyalists joined Loyalist military units that supported the British effort. Two significant leaders appeared, both in New York. One was Guy Johnson, nephew of Sir William Johnson, who had long been the British representative to the Iroquois peoples of New York. Guy Johnson, who gained his uncle's post when the latter died in 1774, worked well with the Indian leader Joseph Brant.

Another effective Loyalist military leader was John Butler. He organized a unit called "Butler's Rangers" that took part in the frontier warfare in western New York and Pennsylvania.

Guy Johnson served in the French and Indian War and led Loyalist attacks on Patriot settlements during the American Revolution. As superintendent of Indian affairs for the British throughout the war, he had close relations with the peoples of the Iroquois Confederacy.

CHAPTER FIVE

British Political Leaders

While the battles of the Revolution were fought on American soil, political leaders far away in Britain had an enormous impact on the course of events. Members of the British government set the military policy, acting under the watchful eye of the king, George III.

King George III

Britain and its empire in the 1700s were governed by a monarchy, which means that a king or queen ruled the nation. George III took the throne as king in 1760 at the age of twenty-two. Beginning in 1765, he suffered from a disease called porphyria, which caused bouts of insanity and eventually made him completely insane and unable to rule.

George III believed deeply in the authority of the British Crown over the colonies. He was outraged by the colonists' protests against British laws and by their insistence on their rights. The king believed it was his duty to keep the British Empire in one piece, and for many years he refused to accept the idea that the colonies should become independent. His determination to punish the rebellious colonists helped make the struggle for U.S. independence long and hard.

The Prime Minister

Britain's monarch appointed an individual to be prime minister, the person who led the British government. The first ten years of George III's rule were fairly chaotic, with seven different men serving as prime minister. This lack of consistent

It was only with great reluctance that King George III eventually accepted the reality of U.S. independence. This print shows him receiving John Adams, the new nation's first ambassador to Britain, in 1785.

leadership contributed to the problems and resentment that arose in the American colonies in the 1750s and 1760s.

In 1770, the king finally found a prime minister he had confidence in: Frederick, Lord North. North led the British government during the American Revolution until March 1782. He did not agree with the king that a forceful response would solve the troubles in America, and he advised a policy that mixed strength with more friendly gestures. But when George III insisted on severe measures, North carried out the king's wishes. North tried to resign several times, but the king always begged him to remain in office.

Government Ministers

The prime minister chose the ministers who ran the various departments

Not the Right Man

"Your Majesty's service requires a man of great abilities, and who is confident of his abilities, who can choose decisively, and carry his determination authoritatively into execution. . . . I am certainly not such a man."

Prime minister Frederick North, letter to King George III during the American Revolution

Frederick, Lord North (1732–1792)

Frederick North was the son of an earl. Educated at Oxford University, he was elected to Parliament when only twenty-two years old. In just five years, he was appointed to a post in one of the ministries. In 1767, North became Chancellor of the Exchequer, the minister responsible for collecting the government's revenues and spending its money.

Three years later, King George III chose North as prime minister. North was a strong speaker and a skilled politician. He was worn down by the war, however, and he was relieved to resign in 1782. In the late 1780s, after losing his sight, North retired from politics.

of government, or ministries. These ministers included several secretaries of state, who carried out British foreign policy; the First Lord of the Admiralty, who oversaw the navy; the Lord Chancellor, in charge of the legal system; and others.

During the Revolution, George, Lord Germain, played a key role in British decisions about the conflict. As secretary of state for the colonies, he was in charge of the conduct of the war in North America.

Poor Relations

Germain favored a strong military response, but his own actions hampered the effort. He did not get along well with John Montagu, the Earl of Sandwich, who controlled the British navy. Germain's constant criticism of the navy and its admirals led to a lack of cooperation between the navy and the army.

In addition, Germain did not do an effective job of coordinating army operations. In 1777, for instance, he approved General John Burgoyne's plan to mount an attack from Canada down the Hudson River to try to split New England from the rest of the states. But he did not make General William Howe—who had troops in New York City—move some of his army north to meet Burgoyne. This lack of action compromised Burgoyne's plan. Until the end of the war, Germain and his commanders had poor relations, which harmed the British war effort.

Finish the Rebellion

"As there is not common sense in protracting a war of this sort, I should be for exerting the utmost force of this kingdom to finish the rebellion in one campaign."

Secretary of State for the Colonies George Germain, on military policy in America, September 1775

Parliament and Congress

When U.S. leaders met at the Constitutional Convention in 1787, an important part of their work was to decide the structure of a new government. What they created resembled Parliament, the legislative branch of the British government, which, like Congress, is divided into two houses. Laws had to be passed by both houses of Parliament to become law, as they did in Congress. The House of Lords was equivalent to the U.S. Senate, and, like the Senate when Congress first came into being, its members were unelected. (Senate members were chosen by state legislators, while members of the House of Lords inherited their seats). The House of Commons, like the House of Representatives, had members elected by voters to represent their specific districts.

The Opposition

The prime minister had to have the support of Parliament to pursue his policies. Throughout most of the war, North enjoyed a substantial majority. As late as 1780, only about 100 of Parliament's nearly 560 members opposed the government's policies. Some powerful voices in Parliament, however, opposed government actions toward the American colonies from the beginning.

William Pitt, a former prime minister who had led the British government during the French and Indian War, was one of these voices. In 1775, he tried to prevent a full-fledged war by offering a plan of compromise. Pitt's idea was to allow the Americans to govern themselves through the Continental Congress while remaining within the British Empire. North's government rejected that idea. As the war continued, Pitt argued against the government's policies. After the British defeat in the Second Battle of Saratoga in late 1777, he warned the government: "You cannot conquer America."

Another critic of the government was Edmund Burke. In 1775, Burke pointed to the value of trade with the colonies and urged a peaceful policy instead of war. He consistently opposed British policies before the war and attacked the government's conduct once the war began.

Force Failing

"The use of force alone is but temporary. It may subdue for a moment; but it does not remove the necessity of subduing again. . . . If you do not succeed, you are without recourse: for, conciliation failing, force remains; but, force failing, no further hope of reconciliation is left."

Philosopher and politician Edmund Burke, speech in the House of Commons, March 22, 1775

Time to Give Up

Eventually, even the war's supporters realized it was time to give up. Approval for the fighting in America quickly evaporated after the surrender of Charles Cornwallis's large British army at Yorktown, Virginia, in October 1781. North resigned the following March, and a new government—determined to make peace with the Americans—was formed. Charles, Lord Rockingham, was appointed prime minister, but he died on July 1, 1782, and was succeeded by William, Lord Shelburne.

In 1782, negotiations began in Paris, France, between the British and Americans for a treaty that would end the war and recognize U.S. independence. In 1783, Shelburne's government signed the Treaty of Paris.

A British cartoon from the 1770s pokes fun at the arguments among British politicians during the American Revolution. While they argue, a map of North America on the wall bursts into flames.

CHAPTER SIX

British Military Leaders

The British had strong, well-trained military forces and several skilled leaders, giving them advantages during the Revolution. Their strategy for winning the war, however, was based on faulty judgment, including beliefs about the help they would get from Loyalists (which was less than they believed) and the determination of the Patriots (which was greater than they thought).

The Commanders

Most of the top commanders in the British army and navy came from the same noble class that dominated the government. Admiral Richard Howe was a viscount. General Charles Cornwallis was an earl. Others, such as Thomas Gage, also came from aristocratic families. A few admirals in the Royal Navy were exceptions. They had come from ordinary families, entered the service when young, and risen through the ranks.

Commanders in Chief

The British appointed military commanders in chief in America before and during the American Revolution. Thomas Gage served in this post from April 1763 to April 1776. He was followed by General William Howe, who turned over command to General Henry Clinton in May 1778. Four years later, as the war was winding down, Clinton was succeeded by General Guy Carleton, who served from 1782 to 1783.

Long-Distance Orders

These generals had overall command of the army, but any plans they devised for major operations

Thomas Gage was military commander in chief in America when the Revolution began. A British cartoon of 1774, showing him thrown off his horse, reflects the problems he faced in dealing with the rebellion in the colonies.

had to be approved by Lord Germain in Britain. Just as often, Germain sent his own plans of action to the commanders in America. This meant that the direction of the war was being determined by someone nearly 3,500 miles (5,600 kilometers) away. In addition, communications took weeks to travel between America and Britain by ship. These delays made it hard to run an effective campaign.

Another problem was that officers under the commander in chief had their own channels of communication to officials in London. They used their personal connections to push their own ideas or pet projects. In 1777, for instance, General John Burgoyne urged Germain to agree to an invasion of New York from Canada without the knowledge of General Howe. And in 1780, Germain sent orders directly to General Charles Cornwallis without consulting Clinton. Such problems in communication caused poor decisions to be made and on occasion contributed to British defeats.

Leave Me to Myself
"If you wish me to do anything, leave me to myself, and let me adapt my efforts to the hourly change of circumstances. If not, tie me down to a certain point and take the risk of my want of success."

General Henry Clinton, letter to George Germain, secretary of state for the colonies, May 1779

Richard Howe (1726–1799) and William Howe (1729–1814)

Richard and William Howe, the second and third sons of a viscount, were both British military leaders during the American Revolution. Richard joined the navy at fourteen, and William joined the army at seventeen. William performed extremely well in several battles during the French and Indian War and won great respect for his courage and leadership. He became a general in 1772. His brother reached the rank of admiral three years later. Both brothers were also members of Parliament and opposed the government's colonial policies of the 1760s and 1770s.

William Howe

When he was sent to America to fight the Patriots, Richard insisted on being given the opportunity to offer a peace settlement, although the effort failed. William Howe captured New York City in 1776 and Philadelphia in 1777, but he failed to destroy Washington's Continental army. Early in 1778, William resigned as commander in chief and returned to Britain. The admiral followed him soon after.

The brothers' conduct of the war became a subject of a debate between the government—which tried to blame them for Britain's defeat at Saratoga in 1777—and their supporters. Parliament launched an investigation, but it was never completed. Admiral Howe later performed brilliantly against the French in 1793, but General Howe did not lead troops in combat again.

Richard Howe

Serving My Country

"My going [to America] was not of my seeking. I was ordered, and could not refuse, without incurring the odious name of backwardness to serve my country in distress."

General William Howe, explaining why he accepted duty in America even though he opposed the war policy, February 21, 1775

Uncertain Aims

Patriot leader George Washington knew what he was trying to do—keep his army alive so as to keep the dream of independence alive. British leaders in the American Revolution, however, had varying goals at different times and places. They were uncertain whether they were aiming to punish the colonies, rally Loyalists to their side, seize territory, or influence people's attitudes. They did all those things at various points in the conflict but still failed to win a victory.

Reducing Resources

After the 1778 alliance between the Patriots and France, the British made a strategic change that doomed their military effort. France was now at war with Britain, not just in America but around the world. Ministers and military leaders were concerned about

French attacks on the wealthy British colonies in the West Indies. They also worried about a possible invasion of Ireland or even Britain itself.

These concerns meant that the British diverted troops and ships to areas other than America. Winning the American Revolution had become less urgent than protecting other possessions, and resources available for fighting the Patriots were reduced.

Because reinforcements were hard to come by, British generals were reluctant to engage in major battles. They feared seeing their forces weakened by heavy **casualties**. For this reason, they did not mount major attacks, nor did they try to destroy Washington's army.

Lack of Cooperation

The British military effort was hampered by a lack of cooperation

Changed Objective

"The object of the war being now changed, and the contest in America being a secondary consideration, our principal object must be distressing France and defending . . . His Majesty's possessions."

Communication to Admiral Richard Howe from the British government, March 22, 1778

General Burgoyne's ships and troops left Canada in June 1777 as part of a plan for cutting off New England from the rest of the United States. The plan relied on the involvement of General Howe's troops, but Howe had plans to capture Philadelphia instead.

between leaders. In 1775, General Gage rejected General Clinton's plans for breaking the siege of Boston by moving south of the city, and instead he attacked Bunker Hill. That attack cost the British hundreds of casualties. In 1777, General Howe refused to cooperate with General Burgoyne's plan to isolate New England and thereby weaken the Patriots, and Burgoyne's plan failed.

The army and navy did not work well together either. The British did not make effective use of their control of the sea before the French, with their large fleet, entered the war. They could have used the Royal Navy to launch multiple attacks, landing troops in many ports at once. Or they could have used ships to move troops quickly from one place to another, seizing key points before the Patriots could march their armies into position. They did neither.

Leadership in Battle

British leaders may have lacked cooperation, an efficient command structure, and clear objectives, but they could be brave in action. They were also very disciplined, on and off the battlefield, and had a highly developed sense of duty to their country.

General William Howe took part in the attack on Patriot lines at the Battle of Bunker Hill in June 1775. He promised his men that he would not make them go any further "than where I go myself at your head." Howe fulfilled his pledge, taking the lead in all three assaults on the Patriot lines despite the heavy casualties around him.

British generals were also skilled in battlefield tactics. Howe outmaneuvered Washington at the Battle of Long Island in August 1776 and at the Battle of Brandywine in September 1777. He was not the only commander to show bravery and skill. General Cornwallis was at the head of British troops who fought fiercely in the Battle of Monmouth in 1778. And Cornwallis brilliantly planned and carried out the Battle of Camden in 1780.

Native Americans Take Sides

In their struggle to retain control of North America, the British were helped over the years by Native Americans. At the time of the Revolution, Native Americans were losing increasing areas of their homelands to American settlers. Because of these losses, more Native

General Charles Cornwallis had a number of successes in the Revolution, but he was also commander of the British army in the South when it was defeated at the Battle of Yorktown in 1781. This painting by John Trumbull shows Washington riding between the victorious French and American soldiers during the surrender ceremony on October 19. Cornwallis did not attend.

tribes sided with the British than with the Patriots in the hope that a British victory would afford them some protection. (Some tribal chiefs, however, took the American side.) In the South, the Creek and the Cherokee peoples fought against the Patriots. In the North, most of the Iroquois Confederacy tribes did so.

The Iroquois Confederacy

The Iroquois Confederacy was an alliance of six tribes in the New York area that comprised the Mohawk, Oneida, Onondaga, Cayuga, Seneca, and Tuscarora peoples. The alliance had been founded long before the Revolution, primarily to end warfare among the tribes.

At the outset of the conflict, leaders of the Iroquois Grand Council declared the Confederacy would be neutral. Nonetheless, individual tribes joined the fight on opposing sides, and members of the Confederacy found themselves killing each other.

Military Leaders

Two Iroquois leaders emerged as military leaders in support of the British during the American Revolution. The most effective—and feared—was the Mohawk Joseph Brant. A leader of Iroquois troops, Brant joined Loyalists in raids on American settlers in New York and Pennsylvania. After the war, Brant never made peace with the United States. Seneca commander Cornplanter also fought ferociously against the Patriots, but he was eager to negotiate with the new U.S. government after the war.

The leaders who made up the Iroquois Grand Council, shown here in a meeting, were unable to keep their tribes from taking sides in the American Revolution in spite of a declaration of neutrality.

Cornplanter (c. 1740–1836)

Cornplanter—also known as John Abeel, John O'Bail, and Kaintwakon—was born to a Seneca mother in present-day New York. His Dutch father was a trader and gunsmith. Through his mother's family, Cornplanter gained influence in the Seneca tribe. During the American Revolution, he became an Iroquois military leader, leading attacks on Patriot forces and American settlers in New York's frontier areas.

After the Revolution, Cornplanter became a negotiator for the Iroquois people in land treaties with the U.S. government. In this role, Cornplanter granted huge areas of Iroquois homelands to the Americans. Not surprisingly, he became very unpopular with his people as a result. Cornplanter believed, however, that friendship with whites was the best way to protect his people from being completely wiped out. He encouraged President Washington to make treaties and pushed for fair treatment of all Native peoples.

After years as a diplomat, Cornplanter eventually became disenchanted with the government's treatment of his people. He spent his later years near the Allegheny River in Pennsylvania, where he had been given a land grant. After Cornplanter's death, the land was handed down among the Seneca until the last resident left in 1964.

Time Line

1760   George III becomes British king.

1770   Frederick, Lord North, becomes British prime minister.
March 5: Boston Massacre.

1773   December 16: Boston Tea Party.

1774   September 5: First Continental Congress opens in Philadelphia.

1775   April: American Revolution begins with Battle of Lexington and Concord, Massachusetts.
June 15: Second Continental Congress appoints George Washington as commander of the Continental army.
June 17: Battle of Bunker Hill, Massachusetts.

1776   January: Thomas Paine's *Common Sense* is published.
July 4: Congress approves Declaration of Independence.
August 27: Battle of Long Island, New York.
December 26: Washington captures Trenton, New Jersey, from the British.

1777   January 3: Washington captures Princeton, New Jersey, from the British.
August: Battle of Bennington, New York (near Bennington, Vermont).
September 11: Battle of Brandywine, Pennsylvania.
October 17: British surrender to Patriots at Saratoga, New York.

1778   February 6: United States and France sign treaty of alliance.
June 28: Battle of Monmouth, New Jersey.
Winter: Friedrich von Steuben begins training Continental troops at Valley Forge, Pennsylvania.

1780   August: Patriots are defeated at Battle of Camden, South Carolina.

1781   Summer: Washington and Comte de Rochambeau plan combined attack on British forces in Virginia.
October 19: British army surrenders to Patriots at Yorktown, Virginia.

1782   Lord North resigns as prime minister.

1783   Treaty of Paris formally ends American Revolution.

1787   May 25: Constitutional Convention opens in Philadelphia.

1789   Washington becomes first U.S. president.

1799   Washington dies.

1826   July 4: Thomas Jefferson dies; John Adams dies.

Glossary

besiege: mount a siege, a military operation in which a group of attackers surrounds a target and either attacks it or keeps it trapped in an attempt to make it surrender.

boycott: refuse to buy goods from or do business with a particular business or country in protest at its policies.

casualty: soldier or other person who is wounded, killed, or missing in battle.

colony: settlement, area, or country owned or controlled by another nation.

congress: meeting. The name "Congress" was given to the first meetings of delegates from the British colonies and was then adopted as the name of the U.S. legislature when the United States formed a national government.

constitution: document that lays down the basic rules and laws of a nation or organization.

court-martial: try a member of a military force in a court of law.

delegate: person chosen to represent a group at a meeting or in making decisions.

Enlightenment: intellectual movement of the 1600s and 1700s that valued reason, individual liberties, and the right of the people to determine their own form of government.

federal: having to do with the whole nation rather individual states. Federal taxes are taxes paid to the U.S. government.

legislature: group of officials that makes laws.

loot: steal or take things by force.

Loyalist: American who rejected independence and wanted the colonies to remain British.

militia: group of citizens organized into an army (as opposed to an army of professional soldiers, or regulars).

Patriot: American who supported the American Revolution; more generally, a person who is loyal to and proud of his or her country.

philosopher: person who studies and develops ideas about topics such as morality, truth, and the meaning of life.

policy: plan or way of doing things.

regiment: unit in an army made up of a varying number of companies. Several regiments make a brigade.

republic: nation that is led by elected officials and that has no monarch.

strategy: overall plan of action during a war.

surveyor: person who measures land, works out boundaries, and makes records of information about land.

tar and feather: apply hot tar and feathers to people's bodies as a form of punishment.

tax: sum charged by the government on purchases, property ownership, or income and used to pay for public services or the cost of governing.

Further Resources

Books

Davis, Kenneth C. *Thomas Jefferson* (Don't Know Much About). Harper Trophy, 2005.

Fleming, Candace. *Ben Franklin's Almanac: Being a True Account of the Good Gentleman's Life*. Atheneum/Anne Schwartz, 2003.

Haugen, Daniel. *Speechmakers and Writers* (Voices from the Revolution). Blackbirch, 2004.

Schmittroth, Linda. *American Revolution Biographies* (American Revolution Reference Library). UXL, 2000.

Wukovits, John F. *Generals of the Revolutionary War* (American War Library). Greenhaven, 2003.

Places to Visit

Boston National Historic Park
Charlestown Navy Yard
Boston, MA 02129
Telephone: (617) 242-5642

Web Sites

George Washington's Mount Vernon Estate and Gardens
www.mountvernon.org
Web site of George Washington estate in Virginia offers information about Washington and his life there.

The George Washington Papers at the Library of Congress – Time Line: The American Revolution
memory.loc.gov/ammem/gwhtml/ gwtimear.html
The Library of Congress presents a time line of Washington's life that includes illustrations and links to original documents. Other sections of the time line cover Washington's life before and after the Revolution.

People of the Revolution
www.si.umich.edu/spies/people.html
As part of its online exhibtion of letters from the Sir Henry Clinton Collection, the William L. Clements Library at the University of Michigan offers biographies of many important Revolutionary figures—from Patriot leaders to French and British officers—and links to their correspondence.

Index